# The Battle of

# Lexington

## A Sermon &

## Eyewitness Narrative

# THE BATTLE

## OF

# LEXINGTON

### A SERMON &

### EYEWITNESS NARRATIVE

BY

## JONAS CLARK
PASTOR

APRIL 19, 1776

Nordskog
Publishing Inc.

Ventura, California
2007

*The Battle of Lexington:*
*A Sermon & Eyewitness Narrative*
Pastor Jonas Clark

Original Title:
*The Fate of Blood-thirsty Oppressors, and*
*GOD's Tender Care of His Distressed People,* 1776

Including poems
*Paul Revere's Ride,* Henry Wadsworth Longfellow
*Lexington,* Oliver Wendell Holmes
*Lexington,* John Greenleaf Whittier
*Concord Hymn,* Ralph Waldo Emerson

Republished by

© 2007 by Nordskog Publishing, Inc.
Second Printing, August 2010
Third Printing, August 2013
Fourth Printing, July 2015
Fifth Printing, July 2019

International Standard Book Number: 978-0-9796736-3-4
Library of Congress Control Number: 2007935667

Theological Editor: Rev. Christopher Hoops
Cover Design by Forge Toro—a composite of two 19th
century engravings of Revolutionary War scenes.
Editing & Book Design: Desta Garrett
Copyediting: Kimberley Winters
*Unless otherwise indicated, Scripture quotations are from:*
Holy Bible, The King James Authorized Version
Text has been kept as true to Pastor Clark's original as possible.

Printed in the United States of America by Printing Partners

Nordskog Publishing, Inc.
2716 Sailor Avenue
Ventura, California 93001, USA
1-805-642-2070 • 1-805-276-5129
NordskogPublishing.com

Member,

**Christian**
**Indie Publishing**
**Association**

# Contents

# The Rev. Christopher Hoops

*Founding Theology Editor,* Nordskog Publishing

(1950–2008)

As a student at San Bernardino Bible College, Chris Hoops began making missionary field trips to the Navajo and Hopi reservations, partnering with local missionaries. After graduation he was asked to teach Old Testament history and minor prophets at his alma mater (1976–1980).

In 1979, Hoops co-founded the Inland Christian Center Academy and served as principal and administrator. In 1980, he moved to Arizona for one year to help missionary friends teach Bible and theology to Navajo and Hopi students.

From 1981–1984 Hoops traveled around the country, lecturing on the need for home schooling, for teaching America's Christian History, and for recovering the contribution of Christianity to Western civilization. These activities led to his founding of American Heritage Christian Church (Camarillo, California), where from 1984–1991, he continued to hold seminars and conferences on those topics.

In 1994, Hoops founded Christ Reformed Church (Colville, Washington) and in 1999 he founded Emanuel Presbyterian Church of Colville and led them into joining the Orthodox Presbyterian Church. In 2001 Hoops moved back to California and took a position at Monte Vista Christian School (Watsonville) teaching Bible to middle and high school students.

He and his wife, Gail, raised three children (a daughter and two sons) and then adopted three daughters in Roseville.

Rev. Hoops was a leader in the Reformed Christian faith, Founding Biblical-Theological Editor for Nordskog Publishing, and was first on the waiting list for his second liver transplant when the Lord took him home.

# The Battle of Lexington

Have you ever wondered who fired the "shot heard 'round the world" that fateful morning of April 19, 1775? Who were those brave men who stood against the best-trained army in the world? The following is Jonas Clark's Sermon on the one-year anniversary and his eyewitness narrative of those events.

None other but Jonas Clark could give such an accounting, for he was the pastor of those "embattled farmers" who stood their ground. Clark is herein giving an honest and accurate accounting of the Battle of Lexington. He is also giving testimony of the events of April 19 and answers the great question, "Who fired the first shot?"

There was no better-prepared place to inaugurate the first battle of the War for Independence than the little village of Lexington. For pastor Clark "discussed from the pulpit the great questions at issue, and that powerful voice thundered forth the principles of personal, civil, and religious liberty, and the right of resistance, in tones as earnest and effective as it had the doctrines of salvation by the cross." (J. T. Headley, *Heroes of Liberty: Chaplains and Clergy of the American Revolution*, 1861, 21.) "It was to the congregation, educated by such a man, that Providence allowed to be entrusted the momentous events of April 19, events which were to decide the fate of a continent—that of civil liberty the world over." (Headley, 23)

Today, the Battle of Lexington is little spoken of, for as a nation we have forgotten our history. We have neglected the heroes of our freedom and liberty. But there was a time when this day was remembered and odes were written to commemorate the occasion. *Paul Revere's Ride* and the *Concord Hymn* are two examples. (See Appendix, pages 75–88.)

Our history books no longer tell the true story of Lexington, so we must.

America is perishing for the need of preachers who apply God's holy Word to every area of life including personal, civil, and religious liberty. The Church needs more pastors like Jonas Clark, a preacher who taught the great doctrines of salvation in Christ alone and the Biblical right to resistance, which gave his congregation courage to stand in the face of great odds. The Battle of Lexington should inspire every man, in all stations of life, to stand and make a difference.

—The Rev. Christopher Hoops, *Roseville, California*

Colonial militia Minuteman

# Background of
# Pastor Jonas Clark

## 1755–1805

The Rev. William Ware, Cambridge, MA, in the *Annals of the American Pulpit*, August 10, 1850, provided insights into the background of Rev. Jonas Clark. I have selected what I feel our readers should know concerning the unique and gifted pastor who was providentially set in Lexington for *just such a time as this*—the incidents which occurred on the green at Lexington that eventful day which led to the Declaration of Independence and the founding of a nation, one nation under God.

Jonas Clark was born on Christmas day, marking his life in obedience to Jesus Christ. He had six sons and six daughters, all but four living at the time of his death. Four of his daughters married clergymen.

Rev. Clark graduated from Cambridge in 1752 and was ordained in Lexington three years later. In addition to being a fulltime clergyman, he was an industrious, hard-working farmer as well. He cultivated sixty acres of land, which he still owned at the end of his life.

As the pastor of the church at Lexington, he typically gave four sermons a week, written out and orally presented—nearly 2200 sermons in his lifetime. His preaching was vigorous in style, animated in manner, instructive in matter, and delivered with uncommon energy and zeal, with an agreeable and powerful voice. His sermons were rarely less than an hour, often more, and in theological opinions he was considered amongst the Trinitarians and Calvinists.

The spirit and temper of his life were just what the Gospel was designed to produce. He was a Christian in the highest and best sense of the term, shown to be such by a long and exemplary life and a faithful practice of the virtues he had preached to others. He was considered a patriot of the most ardent and decided character.

And at Lexington, he witnessed the first outbreak of the War for Independence. The Rev. William Ware wrote a little less than a hundred years later:

It can be regarded only as a singularly happy circumstance that, as Lexington was to be the place where resistance to the power of England was first to occur, and the great act of a declaration of war first to be made by the act of the people in the blood to be there shed, making the place forever famous in history, the minister of Lexington should have been a man of the principles, character, courage, and energy of Mr. Clark.

It can be regarded he was eminently a man produced by the times—more than equal to them; rather a guide and leader. All his previous life, his preaching, his intercourse and conversation among his people had been but a continued and most effectual preparation for the noble stand taken by his people on the morning of the 19th of April, 1775. The militia on the Common that morning were the same who filled the pews of the meetinghouse on the Sunday morning before, and the same who hung upon the rear of the retreating enemy in the forenoon and throughout the day. They were only carrying the preaching of many previous years into practice.

It would not be beyond the truth to assert that there was no person at that time and in that vicinity—not only no clergyman but no other person of whatever calling or profession, who took a firmer stand for the liberties of the country, or was more ready to perform the duties and endure the sacrifices of a patriot, than the minister of Lexington.

When the struggle actually commenced, the people were ready for it, thoroughly acquainted with the reasons on which the duty of resistance was founded, and prepared to discharge the duty at every hazard. No population within the compass of the Colonies were better prepared for the events of the 19th of April, than the people of Lexington; no people to whom the events of that day could more safely have been entrusted; none more worthy of the duties that fell to their lot; or who better deserved the honours which have followed the faithful performance of them. No single individual probably did so much to educate the people up to that point of intelligence, firmness, and courage, as their honoured and beloved pastor.

It was a heavy day to the pastor, who, on the retreat of the British, visiting the grounds directly under the windows of his church, found eight of his beloved parishioners lying dead, and many others wounded. Of the transactions of that morning and day, Jonas Clark drew up a narrative, included as part of his anniversary sermon, which we have republished in this book.

—Gerald Christian Nordskog, *Publisher*

*The Fate of Blood-thirsty Oppressors, and GOD's tender Care of his distressed People.*

A

# S E R M O N,

PREACHED AT LEXINGTON,

April 19, 1776.

To commemorate the *MURDER, BLOOD-SHED* and *Commencement of Hostilities,* between *Great-Britain* and *America,* in that Town, by a Brigade of Troops of GEORGE III. under Command of *Lieutenant-Colonel SMITH,* on the Nineteenth of APRIL, 1775.

TO WHICH IS ADDED,

A BRIEF NARRATIVE of the principal Transactions of that Day.

## By JONAS CLARK, A. M.

PASTOR of the CHURCH in LEXINGTON.

Those Things doth the LORD hate :—*A proud Look, a lying Tongue,* and *Hands that shed innocent Blood.* PROV. VI. 16, 17.
—————and are motives I believe it, Sc.

14679
Clarke, Jonas, 1730-1805.
The Fate of Blood-Thirsty Oppressors.

MASSACHUSETTS-STATE: BOSTON:
PRINTED BY POWARS AND WILLIS.
M,DCC,LXXVI.

*The Fate of Blood-Thirsty Oppressors, and GOD's Tender Care of His Distressed People.*

# A

# S E R M O N,

## Preached at Lexington,

### April 19, 1776

To commemorate the *MURDER, BLOODSHED and Commencement of Hostilities*, between *Great-Britain* and *America*, in that Town, by a Brigade of Troops of George III, under Command of *Lieutenant-Colonel SMITH*, on the Nineteenth of April, 1775.

TO WHICH IS ADDED,

A Brief NARRATIVE of the principal Transactions of that Day.

BY JONAS CLARK, A.M.

PASTOR OF THE CHURCH IN LEXINGTON

(1730–1805)

*Those Things doth the LORD hate:—A proud Look, a lying Tongue, and Hands that shed innocent Blood.* Prov. 6:16–17

MASSACHUSETTS-STATE: BOSTON;

PRINTED BY POWARS AND WILLIS

1776

## A Sermon

*The Fate of Blood-Thirsty Oppressors, and GOD's
Tender Care of His Distressed People.*

JOEL 3:19, 20 & 21

EGYPT *shall be a desolation, and* EDOM *shall be a desolate
wilderness, for the violence against the children of Judah,
because they have shed* INNOCENT BLOOD *in their land.
But* Judah *shall dwell forever, and* Jerusalem *from
generation to generation. For I will cleanse their blood
that I have not cleansed; for the* LORD *dwelleth in Zion.*

N EXT to the acknowledgement of the
existence of a Deity, there is no one
principle of greater importance in
religion than a realizing belief of
the Divine government and providence
as superintending the affairs of the
universe and intimately concerned in
whatever happens to mankind, both as nations and
kingdoms, and as individuals.

Deeply to be impressed with a sense of the divine
providence, to realize that GOD is Governor among
the nations, that His government is wise and just,
and that all our times and changes are in His hands
and at His disposal, will have the happiest tendency

to excite the most grateful acknowledgements of His goodness in prosperity, the most cordial resignation to His paternal discipline in adversity, and the most placid composure and equanimity of mind in all the changing scenes of life. Inspired with this divine principle, we shall contemplate, with grateful wonder and delight, the goodness of God in prosperous events, and devoutly acknowledge and adore His sovereign hand in days of darkness and perplexity, and when the greatest difficulties press. This will be a source of comfort and support under private afflictions and trials, and this shall encourage our hope in God and trust in His name, under public calamities and judgments. Yea, however dark and mysterious the ways of providence may appear, yet nothing shall overwhelm the mind or destroy the trust and hope of those that realize the government of Heaven, that realize that an all-wise God is seated on the throne, and that all things are well-appointed for his chosen people—for them that fear Him.

This principle and these sentiments therefore, being of so great use and importance in religion under the various dispensations of providence, one great design of the present discourse is to rouse and excite us to a religious acknowledgement of the hand of God in those distressing scenes of MURDER, BLOODSHED and WAR, we are met to commemorate upon this solemn occasion.

The passage before us, it is humbly conceived, is well-suited to confirm our faith, to excite our trust and encourage our hope under such awful dispensations, as it points out the method of God's government and the course of His providence towards the enemies and oppressors of His people, and the fate of those that shed *innocent blood;* and at the same time, represents His peculiar care of His church and chosen and the assurance they have when under oppression, of restoration and establishment, and that *God himself* will plead their cause and both *cleanse* and *avenge* their *innocent blood*. "*Egypt* shall be a desolation and *Edom* shall be a desolate wilderness, for the *violence* against the *children of Judah*, because they have shed INNOCENT BLOOD *in their land*. But *Judah* shall dwell forever, and *Jerusalem* from generation to generation. For *I will cleanse their blood*, that I have not cleansed; for the LORD dwelleth in Zion."

It is not necessary to enquire as to the immediate occasion or literal fulfillment of the prophecy before us with respect to the particular nations or kingdoms here mentioned. It is sufficient to our present purpose to observe that *Egypt* was early noted in scripture history for oppressing God's people and causing them to serve with *cruel bondage*. *Edom* also is mentioned as guilty of *violence* towards them and expressing a most embittered hatred and revenge against them; and from the expressions in the text, it is natural to suppose that there had been some, if not many, instances of their shedding *innocent blood* in their land. (Joel 3:19–21; see also Psalm 137:7) *Israel*, God's chosen people had often suffered violence from both these states: so that we have good reason to suppose that both *Egypt* and *Edom*, in the language of scripture prophecy, in the text and other passages, may intend not *Egypt* or *Edom* only, but (proverbially) in a more general sense, enemies, persecutors or oppressors of God's people, who violated their rights and liberties, religious and civil, and by the sword of persecution or oppression shed *innocent blood* in their land.

Prophecies, especially those that are or may be of general use to the people of God, are but seldom literal, either in prediction or fulfillment. They are rather of use to foreshow great and interesting events as taking place in the world in such time and manner, and upon such persons, societies, nations, or kingdoms as shall display the justice and equity of divine government and the peculiar care which Heaven takes of the church and people of God for their correction, instruction, preservation or establishment. Agreeably, St. Paul speaks strongly for this method of explaining and improving scripture prophecies, where he says expressly that "no prophecy of the scripture is of any private interpretation." (2 Peter 1:20) It is therefore rational to suppose that, though prophecies may have special or immediate reference to particular persons, societies, nations or kingdoms and to events in which they may be immediately interested, yet they may be fitly considered as having a further and more important interpretation, which may be of general use for the direction and edification of God's church and people in all ages to the end. In this general sense, therefore, you will permit me to consider the prophecy in the passage before us: and thus understood, it is easy to see several things suggested in it worthy of our most serious attention and religious improvement upon such an occasion as this.

In the first place, it is admitted that for wise purposes, a just God may permit powerful enemies or oppressors to injure, do violence unto and distress His people, and to carry their measures of violence and oppression to such lengths among them, as to strike at their life and "shed *innocent blood* in their land."

As God is the Sovereign of the world and exercises His government for the glory of His name in the good of the whole, so He hath a paternal concern for the special benefit and improvement of His church and people. All creatures are His servants; and God accomplisheth His designs and carries His counsels to effect by what means and instruments He pleases. It is with Him alone, "Who is wonderful in counsel and excellent in working," to bring good out of evil. When God designs the reproof and correction of His people, He can exercise this holy discipline in various ways and by various means as shall best answer the purposes of His government. This holy discipline is accordingly exercised, sometimes by the immediate hand of providence: as in wasting sickness, parching drought, awful and desolating earthquakes or other judgments which are immediately from God Himself. Or this may be done more immediately by the instrumentality of His creatures; and even the wicked and those that love the wages of unrighteousness, that delight in oppression, waste and spoil or thirst for *innocent blood*, may be improved as the rod in His hand to correct or punish the sins of His people. With this view, the oppressor is permitted to injure, insult, oppress and lay waste in a land, and to carry his measures to the shedding of *innocent blood*. With the same design does a sovereign God give the enemy a commission in war, with fire and sword, to distress and destroy.

In such public calamities, it is true it often comes to pass that, as individuals, the innocent are involved and suffer with the guilty and sometimes the innocent alone. But however unjust or cruel the oppressor and those who thirst for blood may be in contriving and carrying into execution their wicked, oppressive, or *bloody* designs, they are no other than instruments in providence and the rod in the hand of the great Governor of the world for the reproof and correction of His people. These things happen not by accident or chance, but by the direction or permission of that God who is righteous in all His ways and holy in all His works. When Israel sinned and did evil in the sight of the LORD, it is said, "the anger of the LORD was hot against Israel, and He delivered them into the hands of spoilers that spoiled them, and He sold them into the hands of their enemies round about, and they were greatly distressed." (Judges 2:14–15) Hence also the *Assyrian King* is expressly called "*the rod of* GOD's *anger*," for the correction of His people. (Isaiah 10:5) And thus *Egypt* and *Edom* in the prophecy before us, in committing violence upon the children of *Judah*, and in shedding of *innocent blood* in their land, are held up to view as the rod in GOD's hand for the correction, reproof and instruction of His people. Agreeably, this is the language of a just and faithful GOD in such dispensations: "*hear ye the rod, and who hath appointed it.*" (Micah 6:9)

It matters not, therefore, who are the immediate instruments of violence and oppression, or by whose hands the blood of innocent persons is shed or their substance wasted and habitations destroyed; nor yet from what motives or views such acts of oppression and cruelty are perpetrated with respect to the religious improvement that GOD expects us, or any people, to make of such heavy dispensations. 'Tis GOD and His hand—'tis GOD and His providence which we are first of all concerned to notice, acknowledge and improve. However unjust our sufferings may be from man, yet when we realize the hand of God, the great and wise Governor of the world as concerned herein, silence and submission is our indispensable duty, and no murmur or complaint ought ever to be heard, but with reverence and humility it becomes us to bow before the LORD and, adoring His sovereignty, ascribe righteousness to our GOD. Neither the insults of oppressors nor the flames of our once delightful habitations, nor even the *innocent blood of our brethren slain*, should move to a murmuring word or an angry thought against GOD, His government, or providence. "Shall we receive good at the hand of GOD, and shall we not receive evil?" (Job 2:10) And "shall not the Judge of all the earth do right?" (Genesis 18:25) The more grievously we are smitten, the more deeply we are affected, the more carefully should we endeavour to realize our dependence upon GOD, the more religiously acknowledge His hand and the more earnestly return to Him that smites. This is the lesson of instruction, which GOD expects we should learn by such bitter dispensations, and this the improvement He looks for in us and

His people in order to [receive] the restoration of His favor and our redemption from enemies and oppressors who threaten to lay waste and destroy. May these things, then, be deeply impressed on each of our hearts. But I pass—

Secondly, to observe the fate of oppressors and the sentence of heaven against those that do violence to GOD's people and shed *innocent blood* in their land. *Egypt shall be a desolation, and Edom shall be a desolate wilderness, for the violence against the children of Judah, because they have shed innocent blood in their land.*

However just it may be in GOD to correct His people, and whatever right is ascribed to Him of improving the wicked, as the rod in His hand to correct, or the sword to punish them, yet this alters not the nature of their oppressive designs, neither does it abate their guilt or alleviate their crime in these measures of injustice, violence or cruelty by which the people of GOD are distressed.

Thus GOD speaks of the *Assyrian king*, a prince noted in history for his avarice and ambition, cruelty and oppression, (and in him, of the *Assyrian state*, whose character was included in that of its king) saying, "O Assyrian, the rod of mine anger and the staff in their hand is mine indignation. I will send him to an hypocritical nation; and to the people of my wrath will I give him a charge to take the spoil and to take the prey, and to tread them down like the mire of the streets. Howbeit, he meaneth not so, neither doth his heart think so, but it is in his heart to destroy. Wherefore it shall come to pass, that when the LORD hath performed His whole work upon mount Zion and on Jerusalem, I will punish the fruit of the stout heart of the king of Assyria and the glory of his high looks." (Isaiah 10:5–8, 11–12) And so it came to pass: For this power that with such a mighty hand, and for so long a time, oppressed GOD's people and other nations, in GOD's due time, felt the weight of the iron yoke and received double for all the injustice, oppression and cruelty it had exercised towards others.

In this and many other circumstances with which history abounds, it is easy to see the fate of the enemies of GOD's people and oppressors of mankind. But we need not go from the text for satisfaction in this matter. In the words of the prophecy before us, we have the sentence of heaven against the oppres-

23

sors of GOD's people and the doom of those common enemies of mankind pronounced, and the reason thereof assigned in the cleareſt terms. *Egypt shall be a desolation, Edom shall be a desolate wilderness, for the violence againſt the children of Judah, because they have shed innocent blood in their land.*

The LORD is a GOD that loveth righteousness and hateth inequity, in whatever shape or charaćter it appears. Injuſtice, oppression and violence (much less the shedding of innocent blood) shall not pass unnoticed by the juſt Governor of the world. Sooner or later, a juſt recompence will be made upon such workers of iniquity. Yea, though hand join in hand in measures of oppression and violence againſt GOD's people, and though their avarice, ambition and lawless thirſt for power and domination may carry them on 'till their ſteps shall be marked with *innocent blood*, yet certain it is they shall not finally go unpunished. For a time indeed, and but for a time, such workers of unrighteousness, such deſtroyers of mankind may praćtice and prosper, but "vengeance slow is vengeance sure." Their ways are marked before GOD. Their punishment and deſtrućtion are sealed in His presence, and the time is haſtening when

24

destruction without remedy shall be their portion.

The truth of these sentiments hath often been verified in providence, and the proudest princes and the most powerful states have been taught by severe, by fatal experience, that desolation from the LORD awaits the impiety of those who do violence to His people and "shed *innocent blood* in their land."

Here then we may see the light in which that people or nation are to be considered that walk in the ways of oppression and that thirst for and shed innocent blood. Here we may also see the ruin to which they are hastening, the awful judgments that await them, and the great reason they have to fear the sentence of heaven denounced against them in the prophecy before us and its literal fulfillment upon them; which naturally leads in the last place—

Thirdly, to observe in the prophecy before us, the peculiar care God takes of His Church and people, and the assurance they have, even when actually suffering violence and under the cruel hand of oppression, of redemption, restoration and establishment; and that GOD himself will plead their cause, and both *cleanse* and *avenge* their innocent blood. Nothing can be more directly expressive of this sentiment or a firmer ground of assurance for the confirmation of the faith and hope of GOD's chosen people in the belief of it, than the promise and prophecy concerning *Judah* and *Jerusalem* in the text. While *Egypt* and *Edom*—while the enemies and oppressors of God's people—are doomed to that desolation they so justly deserve, the strongest assurances are given "that *Judah* shall dwell forever, and *Jerusalem* from generation to generation. For I, saith God, will cleanse their blood that I have not cleansed: For the LORD dwelleth in Zion." The words are plain and need no comment. They speak the language of scripture, fact and experience for the confirmation of the faith and hope of God's Church and chosen, in days of perplexity and darkness and when actually under the injustice, violence and cruelty of inveterate enemies or *bloodthirsty* oppressors.

Here are two things for the inducement and confirmation of the faith and hope of God's church and people in such times of darkness and distress, which are well worth serious notice and attention.

First, God's word and promise in which He assures His people that, notwithstanding the violence of their enemy against them and the distress and sorrow their oppressors may have caused them by shedding *innocent blood* among them, they shall never avail to overthrow or destroy them; but assuredly His people shall be redeemed, and restored and established as His church and people in a flourishing state.

And then, secondly, to leave no doubt upon their minds as to the fulfillment of this blessed promise, a gracious God condescends to explain Himself in the clearest terms possible, and to satisfy them that nothing should fail of all that He had promised, He assures them that He would take the work into His own hands and see to the accomplishment of it Himself; that thus it might appear to them and to the world of mankind, that the Lord was with them and dwelt in the midst of them. "*Judah* shall dwell forever and *Jerusalem* from generation to generation: For *I* will cleanse their blood, that I have not cleansed; for *the Lord dwelleth in Zion*," —words well suited to cheer and comfort the sinking spirits of God's afflicted, oppressed people, and words which might rouse the faith and give a spring to the hope of the most feeble and faint-hearted among God's people in the depth of distress. For "God is not a man that He should lie, nor the son of man that He should repent." (Numbers 23:19; see also 1 Samuel 15:29) "Hath He promised, and shall He not perform? Hath He spoken, and shall He not bring it to pass?"

Blood is said to be cleansed, or avenged, when justice hath taken place and the murderer is punished. God may be said to cleanse the innocent blood which may have been shed among his people by the sword of oppressors or enemies, when in providence He undertakes for them, avenges their blood upon them that slew them, and reduces them to reason or ruin.

The sword is an appeal to heaven when, therefore, the arms of a people are eventually successful, or by the immediate interposition of providence their enemies and oppressors are subdued or destroyed. When a people are reinstated in peace, upon equitable terms, and established in the enjoyment of all their just rights and liberties, both civil and sacred, then may it be said that the Lord hath cleansed their innocent blood, and then will it be manifestly evident that their God is with them and dwelleth in the midst of them.

Now, of this, God hath given His people the strongest assurances in the prophecy before us, and these assurances are confirmed by the word of God to His people through the sacred scriptures. So that, though for their sins and the multitude of their transgressions, a righteous God may justly afflict and correct His people by the hand of oppressors and permit their most important rights to be violated, their substance destroyed, their habitations to be laid waste, or even the *innocent blood* of their brethren to be wantonly shed in their land, yet still He is their God in the midst of them and will readily appear for their help when they return from their evil ways, acknowledge His hand and implore His mercy and assistance. This holy discipline is no more than what God hath given His people to expect as a reproof of their declensions and as a means of bringing them to a sense of their dependence upon Him. Such dispensations are so far from being an evidence that God hath forsaken His people, given them up, or forgotten to be gracious, that they are rather to be considered as demonstrations of His paternal care and faithfulness towards them. Agreeably, in His covenant with His servant *David* and His house, this method of conduct is expressly stipulated as a token of His special care and faithfulness and of the remembrance of the covenant He had made. "If his children forsake my law and walk not in my judgments: Then will I visit their transgression with the rod and their iniquity with stripes. Nevertheless, my loving-kindness will I not utterly take from him, nor suffer my faithfulness to fail. My covenant will I not break, nor alter the thing that is gone out of my lips." (Psalm 89:30–34)

In such visitations, God evidently intends the best good of His people; not their destruction but their reformation. And if they see His hand, humble themselves under it and seek him aright, God will not fail to remember His covenant and His promises for them and, in His due time, appear in His power and glory for their relief. Yea, the bowels of His mercy will be moved at their distresses, and His language will be the same as unto His people of old when under the *Egyptian yoke* they were caused to serve with cruel bondage. "I have seen, I have seen the affliction of my people which is in Egypt, and have heard their groaning, and am come down to deliver them." (Acts 7:34) And to encourage His saints and people to trust on His name and hope in His mercy, a gracious God hath most explicitly promised them His presence, direction and assistance in all their distresses, be they ever so numerous, ever so great. His language is merciful, condescending and endearing—especially when by the prophet Isaiah he says to his afflicted people—"When thou passest through the waters, I will be with thee; and through the rivers, they shall not overflow thee: when thou walkest through the fire thou shalt not be burnt; neither shall the flame kindle upon thee. For I am the LORD Thy God, the Holy One of Israel, thy Saviour." (Isaiah 43:2–3a) From these passages of sacred writ it appears that as God in infinite wisdom sees fit to exercise His people with trials and afflictions, and sometimes to call them to pass through the depths of adversity, so he hath provided for their support and given them the greatest reason to hope for His presence and assistance and the strongest assurances that they shall be carried through all and, in the end, rejoice in God, *as the Holy One of Israel, their SAVIOUR*. In short, nothing can be more expressive of God's care of His people in distress and of the solid ground they have to hope for redemption and salvation, in His way and time, which are always the best.

We may add, that further to confirm our faith and

encourage our hope in those blessed assurances of God's presence with His people, even in their heaviest trials and greatest perplexities, we might safely appeal to the experience of His chosen in every age, from the beginning to the present time. This will show how easy it is, with an infinitely wise God, to bring good out of evil and, by the over-ruling hand of Providence, to cause the councils and measures of persecutors and oppressors to hasten the redemption and establishment of the injured and oppressed, as well as to bring upon themselves that confusion and desolation they so justly deserve. And this will also prove how truly applicable the words of the prophet are to God's chosen people in their distresses in every age, when speaking of the large experience Israel had had, of the tender love and faithful care of a merciful God exercised towards them, He says that, "In all their affliction He was afflicted, and the angel of His presence saved them: In His love and in His pity He redeemed them, and He bare them and carried them all the days of old." (Isaiah 63:9)

Nothing is more evident from history and experience than God's care of His people and the wisdom of His providence in causing the violence and oppression of their enemies to operate for their advantage and promote their more speedy deliverance. This appears too plain from various instances to admit of dispute.

The *children of Israel* would not have been so early persuaded to have left the gardens of *Egypt* or the fertile fields of the land of *Goshen* and, in the face of every danger, attempted to free themselves from the *Egyptian* yoke, had not their burdens been increased to an unreasonable degree by the violence and cruelty of those that oppressed them in that house of bondage. And *Pharaoh and his armies* would never have met with that disgraceful defeat and awful destruction which overtook them in the *Red Sea*, had they not been infatuated to pursue their measures of oppression and violence after it was evident that their cause was desperate and that God was against them.

*Christendom* would never have been roused from that state of ignorance and darkness and slavery it was in, the *protestant league* would never been entered into with such firmness and resolution to shake off the *papal yoke* and redeem both *church* and *state* from the *hierarchy of Rome* had not the enormities and violence of that power by which they had been so long oppressed, rose to an intolerable heighth and put them upon the expedient.[1]

The *united states* of *Holland* would not have been very easily induced to have opposed the power of *Spain,* when at the meridian of its strength and glory, much less to have attempted independence of that kingdom, had they not been effectually convinced by a long series of injuries and oppression, and numberless violations of their most sacred rights, that there was no other remedy.[2]

*Britons* would never have resisted their kings and flown to arms in defence of their invaluable rights and liberties had they not felt the weight of the iron rod of oppression and tyranny and seen their danger and the absolute necessity of such resistance to prevent the total deprivation of all they held dear and sacred as *Freemen, Christians* and a *free People. Charles* would not have lost his kingdom and finally his life upon the *Scaffold,* by the hand of the executioner; nor *James* been obliged, in disgrace, to quit his throne and abdicate the government of the kingdom, had it not been for their own violent counsels and measures to oppress and enslave the people whom they were called to govern and protect.

Our *fathers* would never have forsook their native land, delightsome habitations and fair possessions and, in the face of almost every danger and distress, sought a safe retreat for the enjoyment of religious and civil liberty among savage beasts and more savage men in the *inhospitable wilds of America*, had they not been drove from thence by the violence and cruelty of persecutors and oppressors in church and state. The *hierarchy of the church*, by which they looked upon the rights of conscience infringed, and the *arbitrary measures of the state*, by which they esteemed their civil liberties abridged, if not grossly violated, rather than any views of worldly gain (as hath been enviously hinted by some) were the principal causes of their emigration and the hope and expectation of deliverance therefrom gave the spring to the hazardous undertaking.

And when heaven so far smiled upon their enterprise as to give them footing in the land; and when, after numerous hardships and dangers, toils and distresses, they had secured a possession for themselves and posterity, and obtained a confirmation of those civil and religious liberties they had sought, still retaining a filial affection towards their *native country,* they seemed to have nothing more at heart than that *Americans* might be happy in the enjoyment of their just rights and liberties, as men and Christians, under the protection of *Britain*; and that *Britain* might be flourishing and glorious in receiving the profits of the labour, trade and industry of *Americans*; and that the connection of *America* with *Britain* and her dependence in this way upon the *Parent State,* might have been preserved inviolate to the end of time. And it may be added that there is no just ground to suppose that it would have ever entered the heart of *Americans* to have desired a dissolution of so happy a connection with the *Mother Country* or to have sought independence of *Britain,* had they not been urged, and even forced upon, such an expedient by measures of oppression and violence, and *the shedding of innocent blood.*

But, alas! Ill-judged counsels! Ill-fated measures of *Britain* and the *British administration* with respect to *America,* have broken in upon the pleasing scene and fatally destroyed the happy prospects of both *Britain* and *America*!

At the close of the last war, we arrived at that happy period to which our ancestors looked with earnest expectation as the utmost of their wishes as the answer of their prayers and the reward of all their toils and sufferings. The *savages* were subdued, those restless neighbours, the *French*, were subjected, and this wide extended continent seemed to be given us for a possession: And we were ready to say, "there was none to make us afraid." But how uncertain the most blooming prospects? How vain, how disappointing the most *rational*, as well as raised expectations, in this imperfect state? Scarcely emerged from the dangers and fatigues of a long and distressing war, we are unexpectedly involved in perplexities and anxieties of different kinds, which by degrees have increased 'till they are become more serious, dangerous and distressing than any ever yet felt by God's people in this *once* happy land.

Through the crafty insinuations, false representations and diabolical counsels of the enemies of God's people and the common rights of mankind in *America* and *Britain*, *acts of oppression* are made by the *Parliament of England* in which we are not represented, which deeply affect our most valuable privileges. In open violation of our *chartered* rights, these acts of unrighteousness and oppression are attempted to be carried into execution in these *colonies*. After various threats of coercive measures, a *military force* is sent to enforce them. An innocent, loyal people are diſtressed, and every art, which wit or malice could invent, is used to flatter or fright, to divide or dishearten, and finally subjeċt us to the will of a power not known to our *charters* or even in the *Britiſh conſtitution itſelf.* And as one of the natural consequences of *ſtanding armies* being ſtationed in populous cities for such execrable purposes, many of the inhabitants of *Boſton* are insulted. At length, under pretence of ill-treatment, the ſtreets of that once flourishing city are ſtained with the *innocent blood* of a number of our brethren, wantonly or cruelly slain by those sons of oppression and violence![3]

Upon the high resentments of the people in consequence of this *horrid outrage* and *violence*, there was, for a short time, a pause in their measures. For a moment the oppressors themselves seemed to be ſtruck with the horrid effeċts of their own iniquitous proceedings and ſtand *aghaſt* at the sight of the *innocent blood* they had shed! Perhaps they were not at that time so thoroughly hardened in sin as they have proved themselves since! But this pause seemed to be not to repent of their evil deeds, but rather to collect themselves and devise some measures more effectual: For so far from giving over the *execrable* design, the plan of oppression is renewed. *New acts* are passed to distress and enslave us. This lust of domination appears no longer in disguise, but with open face. The *starving Port-Bill* comes forth: *Gage* arrives with his forces by sea and land to carry it into execution with vigor and severity. And to complete the scene and at once to make thorough work of oppression and tyranny, immediately follow *the Bills* that subvert the constitution, vacate our *charter*, abridge us of the right of trial by juries of the vicinity in divers specified capital cases, and expose us to be seized, contrary to the laws of the land, and carried to *England* to be tried for our lives! As also *the Bill* for establishing the *popish* religion in *Canada*, contrary to the faith of the crown and the statutes of the kingdom.

Add to these things, the people are treated in various instances with indignity, severity and even cruelty. And, notwithstanding every possible expression of a peaceful disposition in this people, consistent with a determined resolution and Christian firmness, in defence of their rights and liberties which they held dearer than life, their property is frequently and violently seized, and even their persons and lives are threatened. The inhabitants of *Salem are threatened with the sword*,[4] for peacefully meeting to consult upon matters of importance to themselves and the public, as they had an undoubted right to do by the standing laws of the colony. A number of the most respectable inhabitants of that town were *arrested* and *threatened with imprisonment* by *General Gage's* order, for calling the inhabitants together at the meeting aforesaid. The *province stores of powder,* which were deposited at *Medford,* were also clandestinely seized by a large detachment of the troops and conveyed with all possible dispatch to *Boston,* as *were* at the same time, also, some *field-pieces* at *Cambridge.*[5] Entrenchments are thrown up by *Gage's* army, and the town of *Boston* becomes a garrison, and the inhabitants become prisoners at the pleasure of the troops. And notwithstanding *Gage's* repeated professions of having no design against the lives or liberties of the people, every thing hath the appearance of *hostile intentions* and of the near approach of *bloodshed* and *war.*[6]

Many inhabitants both of the town and country are daily abused and insulted by the troops. The devotion of God's people in their worshipping assemblies is frequently interrupted, and marks of the *utmost contempt* are cast upon religion itself. Bodies of troops from time to time march into the country, with a view (as was supposed) to alarm, terrify, or awe the inhabitants to a submission. On the *Sabbath*, a day held sacred to God and religion by Christians, while God's people were in His house engaged in devotion and the instituted services of religion, a detachment of these instruments of tyranny and oppression clandestinely landed at *Marblehead* and, making a quick march to *Salem*, attempt to seize upon some *cannon* and other military stores deposited there to be ready for use, if wanted upon any important emergency: But happily, they are disappointed in their designs by the spirit and resolution of the inhabitants, who speedily collected upon that alarming occasion.[7]

At length, on the night of the eighteenth of April, 1775, the alarm is given of the hostile designs of the troops. The *militia of this town* is called together to consult and prepare for whatever might be necessary, or in their power, for their own and common safety, though without the least design of commencing hostilities upon these *avowed* enemies and oppressors of their country. In the meantime, under cover of the darkness, a brigade of those instruments of violence and tyranny makes their approach and, with a quick and silent march on the morning of the nineteenth, they enter this town. And this is the place where the fatal scene begins! They approach with the morning light; and, more like *murderers* and *cut-throats* than the troops of a *Christian king*, without provocation, without warning, when no war was proclaimed, they drew the *sword of violence* upon the inhabitants of this town and, with a *cruelty* and *barbarity* which would have made the most hardened savage blush, they *shed INNOCENT BLOOD!* But, O my God! How shall I speak!—or how describe the distress, the *horror* of that *awful morn*, that *gloomy day! Yonder field* can witness the *innocent blood* of our brethren slain![8] And from thence does *their blood* cry unto God for vengeance from the ground! There the tender father bled, and there the beloved son! There the hoary head, and there the blooming youth! And there the man in his full strength with the man of years! *They bleed, they die*, not by the sword of an open enemy (with whom war is proclaimed) in the field of battle, but by the hand of those that delight in spoil and *lurk privily that they may shed innocent blood!* But they bleed, they die, not in their own cause only, but in the cause of this whole people—in the cause of God, their country and posterity. And they have not bled, they shall not bleed, in vain. Surely there is one that avengeth and that will plead the cause of the injured and oppressed; and in His own way and time will both *cleanse and avenge their innocent blood.* And the names of *Munroe, Parker,* and others that fell victims to the rage of *blood-thirsty* oppressors on that gloomy morning, shall be had in grateful remembrance by the people of this land, and transmitted to posterity, with honour and respect throughout all generations.[9]

But who shall comfort the distressed relatives, the mourning widows, the fatherless children, the weeping parents, or the afflicted friends? May the consolations of that God, who hath hitherto supported them, be still their support! Upon Him may they still depend, and from Him and His grace may they still derive all needed supplies, in things spiritual and temporal; and yet more and more experience the faithfulness and truth, the mercy and goodness, of the God of all comfort.

May those that were wounded and have since experienced the tender mercy of that God, "Who woundeth, and healeth, and bindeth up," be deeply impressed with a sense of His distinguishing goodness, that their lives were spared while others were taken; and be persuaded more entirely than ever to devote themselves to God, His service and glory.

May all in this place still carefully remember, notice and improve this awful dispensation. Particularly it concerns, not only those whose substance hath been plundered and whose habitations have been burnt by these lawless invaders, but also all, in general, diligently and seriously to enquire: wherefore it is that a righteous God is contending with us by the *fire* and *sword* of the oppressor; and wherefore it is that this *awful scene of blood-shed and war* was opened in this place. May we still humble ourselves before God under a sense of the *terrible* things which, in righteousness, He hath done in the midst of us. May we also be deeply impressed with a most grateful sense of the goodness of God, in that so much mercy was remembered in judgment, that so few were found among the *wounded* and *slain*, and so few habitations were consumed by the fire of the enemy, when so many were spared that were equally exposed. And may this day be remembered to the glory of God and our own instruction and improvement, so long as we live.

But it is not by us alone that this day is to be noticed. This *ever memorable day* is full of importance to all around, to this whole land and nation; and big with the fate of *Great Britain* and *America*. From this *remarkable day* will an important *era* begin for both *America* and *Britain*. And from the *nineteenth of April, 1775*, we may venture to predict, will be dated in future history THE LIBERTY or SLAVERY of the AMERICAN WORLD, according as a sovereign God shall see fit to smile or frown upon the *interesting cause* in which we are engaged.

How far the prophecy before us may be applicable upon this solemn occasion, and with what degree of truth or probability it may be predicted, in consequence of the present unjust and unnatural war, "that *Great Britain* shall be a desolation and *England* be a desolate wilderness for the *violence* against the *children* of *America*, because they have shed INNOCENT

*BLOOD* in their land: But *America* shall dwell forever, and *this people* from generation to generation. And the Lord Himself *will cleanse their blood*, that He hath not *already cleansed*." How far (I say) this prophecy may be applicable in the present *interesting contest*, and how far it may be accomplished in the issue thereof, God only knows, and time only can discover. But of this we are certain, if we "humble ourselves under the mighty hand of God upon us, we shall be exalted, in His due time;" and if we rightly improve His dealings, "accept the punishment of our sins" and religiously trust in His name, we shall see His salvation.

From what hath already happened in the rise and progress and even unto the present state of this most interesting conflict, we have the greatest reason to hope for an happy issue in the end. Though with *fire* and *sword*, our enemies and oppressors have endeavoured to lay waste and destroy, and though they have begun and carried on the war so far as their power could enable them, with more than savage cruelty and barbarity; yet, through the peculiar favour of heaven they have not been able to carry their designs to effect; yea, in most of their enterprises, they have been greatly disappointed, not to say defeated and disgraced. Instead of awing the people into submission by those measures of violence and cruelty with which they commenced hostilities against us, as they undoubtedly expected, their spirits have been roused and awakened thereby beyond what any other means could have ever effected. And, with a union and firmness exceeding the most sanguine expectations, they have armed to defend themselves and their country and to revenge the injuries received and *the innocent blood of their brethren slain*. And a merciful God in various instances hath crowned our arms with success and victory. Not only the acquisitions at the westward, and the progress of our army in *Canada*, but the preservation and defense of this *colony*; and above all the unexpected evacuation of the *town of Boston*, which at such immense cost they had fortified and had so long in their possession, and their destroying the works of their own hands, which with so much labour and expense they had erected; bespeak the special favour of heaven to this injured and oppressed people; and appear to be happy omens of those further successes which are necessary to complete our deliverance and render this land a quiet habitation.

May that God, who is a God of righteousness and salvation, still appear for us, go forth with our armies, tread down our enemies, and *cleanse* and avenge our *innocent blood*. And may we be prepared, by a general repentance and thorough reformation, for His gracious and powerful interposition in our behalf; and then may we see the displays of His power and glory for our salvation. Which God of His infinite mercy grant, for His mercy's sake in Christ Jesus.

## AMEN

# The Battle of Lexington:

## An Eyewitness

## Narrative

### of

## That Day

### by
# Jonas Clark

Painted by Alonzo Chappel

THE BATTLE OF LEXINGTON

Engraved by J. Smillie

# A Narrative, &c.

*As it was not consistent with the limits of a single discourse to give a full account of the particulars of this* most savage *and murderous affair; the following* plain *and* faithful narrative of facts, *as they appeared to us in this place, may be a matter of satisfaction.*

N the evening of the *eighteenth of April*, 1775, we received two messages: the first verbal, the other *by express, in writing*, from the *committee of safety* who were then sitting in the westerly part of *Cambridge*, directed to the Honorable JOHN HANCOCK, Esq., (who, with the Honorable SAMUEL ADAMS, Esq., was then providentially with us) informing, "that *eight* or *nine officers* of the *king's troops* were seen, just before night, passing the road towards *Lexington*, in a *musing, contemplative* posture, and it was suspected they were out upon some evil design."

As both these gentlemen had been frequently and even *publicly* threatened by the enemies of *this people,* both in *England* and *America,* with the *vengeance of the British administration,* and as *Mr. Hancock* in particular had been more than once personally insulted by some officers of the troops in Boston; it was not without some just grounds supposed that under cover of the darkness, *sudden arrest* if not *assassination* might be attempted by these *instruments of tyranny!*

To prevent anything of this kind, *ten* or *twelve* men were immediately collected, in arms, to guard my house through the night.

In the meantime, said *officers* passed through this town on the road towards *Concord.* It was, therefore, thought expedient to watch their motions and, if possible, make some discovery of their intentions. Accordingly, about 10 o'clock in the evening, three men on horses were dispatched for this purpose. As they were *peaceably* passing the road towards *Concord* in the borders of *Lincoln,* they were suddenly stopped by *said officers,* who rode up to them and putting pistols to their breasts and seizing their horses' bridles, *swore if they ſtirred another ſtep, they should be all dead men!* The officers detained them several hours *as prisoners*, examined, searched, abused and insulted them, and, in their haſty return (supposing themselves discovered), they left them in *Lexington*. Said officers also took into cuſtody, abused and *threatened with their lives* several other persons, some of whom they met peaceably passing on the road, others even at the doors of their dwellings, without the leaſt provocation on the part of the inhabitants or so much as a queſtion asked by them.

Between the hours of *twelve* and *one* on the morning of the *Nineteenth of April,* we received intelligence by express from the Honorable JOSEPH WARREN, Esq. at *Boſton,* "that a large body of the *king's troops* (supposed to be a brigade of about 1200 or 1500) were embarked in boats from *Boſton* and gone over to land on *Lechmere's Point* (so called) in *Cambridge,* and that it was shrewdly suspected that they were ordered to seize and deſtroy the *ſtores belonging to the colony then deposited at Concord,*" in consequence of *General Gage's unjuſtifiable seizure of the provincial magazines of powder at Medford* and other *colony ſtores* in several other places.

Upon this intelligence, as also upon information of the conduct of the officers as above mentioned, the *militia* of this town was alarmed and ordered to meet on the usual place of parade; not with any design of *commencing hostilities* upon the *king's troops,* but to consult what might be done for our own and the people's safety: And also to be ready for whatever service providence might call us out to upon this alarming occasion, in case *overt acts of violence* or *open hostilities* should be committed by this *mercenary band of armed and blood-thirsty oppressors.*

About the same time, two persons were sent express to *Cambridge*, if possible, to gain intelligence of the motions of the troops and what route they took.

The *militia* met according to order; and waited the return of the messengers, that they might order their measures as occasion should require. Between 3 and 4 o'clock, one of the expresses returned, informing that there was no appearance of the troops on the roads, either from *Cambridge* or *Charlestown;* and that it was supposed that the *movements in the army* the evening before were only *a feint* to alarm the people. Upon this, therefore, the *militia company* was dismissed for the present, but with orders to be within call of the drum, waiting the return of the other messenger who was expected in about an hour or sooner, if any discovery should be made of the motions of the troops. But he was prevented by their silent and sudden arrival at the place where he was waiting for intelligence. So that, after all this precaution, we had no notice of their approach 'till the *brigade* was *actually in the town* and, upon a quick march, within about a mile and a quarter of the *meetinghouse* and *place of parade*.

However, the commanding officer thought best to call the company together, not with any design of opposing so superior a force, *much less of commencing hostilities*, but only with a view to determine what to do, when and where to meet, and to dismiss and disperse.

Accordingly, about half an hour after 4 o'clock, *alarm guns were fired and the drums beat to arms;* and the *militia* was collecting together. Some, to the number of about 50 or 60, or possibly more, were on the parade, others were coming towards it. In the meantime, the troops, having thus stolen a march upon us, and to prevent any intelligence of their approach, having seized and held prisoners several persons whom they met *unarmed* upon the road, seemed to come *determined for MURDER* and *BLOODSHED;* and that whether provoked to it, or not! When within about half a quarter of a mile of the *meetinghouse,* they halted and the command was given to *prime* and *load;* which, being done, they marched on 'till they came up to the eaſt end of said meetinghouse, in sight of our *militia* (collecting as aforesaid) who was about 12 or 13 rods diſtant. Immediately upon their appearing so suddenly and *so nigh, Capt. Parker,* who commanded the *militia company,* ordered the men to disperse and take care of themselves, and *not to fire.* Upon this, our men dispersed; but many of them, not so speedily as they might have done, not having the moſt diſtant idea of such *brutal barbarity* and more than *savage CRUELTY* from the troops of a *British KING* as they immediately experienced! For no sooner did they come in sight of our company, but one of them, supposed to be an officer of rank, was heard to say to the troops, *"Damn them; we will have them!"* Upon which the troops shouted aloud, huzza'd, and rushed furiously towards our men. About the same time, three officers (supposed to be *Col. Smith, Major Pitcairn* and another officer) advanced on horseback to the front of the body and, coming within 5 or 6 rods of the *militia*, one of them cried out, *"Ye villains, ye Rebels, disperse; damn you, disperse!"* or words to that effect. One of them (whether the same, or not, is not easily determined) said, *"Lay down your arms; damn you, why don't you lay down your arms!"* The second of these officers about this time fired a pistol towards the *militia* as it was dispersing. The foremost, who was within a few yards of our men, brandishing his sword and then pointing towards them, with a loud voice said to the troops, *"Fire! By God, fire!"* which was instantly followed by a discharge of arms from the said troops, succeeded by a very heavy and close fire upon our party, dispersing, so long as any of them were within reach. *Eight were left dead upon the ground!* [10] *Ten were wounded.* The rest of the company, through divine goodness, were (to a miracle) preserved unhurt in this murderous action!

As to the question, "Who fired first?," if it can be a question with anyone; we may observe, that though *General Gage* hath been pleased to tell the world in his account of this *savage transaction*, "that the troops were fired upon by *the rebels* out of the *meetinghouse* and the *neighbouring houses*, as well as by those that were in the field; and that the troops *only* returned the fire and passed on their way to *Concord*;" yet nothing can be more certain than the contrary, and nothing more *false, weak,* or *wicked* than such a representation.

Thomas Gage, Governor 1774

To say nothing of the absurdity of the supposition, "that 50, 60, or even 70 men, should, in the *open field, commence hoſtilities* with 1200 or 1500 of the beſt troops of *Britain,*"[11] nor of the *known* determination of this small party of *Americans,* upon no consideration whatever, to begin the scene of blood.[12] A cloud of witnesses, whose veracity cannot be juſtly disputed, *upon oath* have declared in the moſt express and positive terms, *"that the British troops fired firſt."*[13] And, I think, we may safely add, without the leaſt reason or provocation. Nor was there opportunity given for our men to have saved themselves, either by laying down their arms or dispersing, as direćted, had they been disposed to; as the command to fire upon them was given almoſt at the same inſtant that they were ordered, by the *British officers,* to *disperse* and to *lay down their arms, &c.*

In short, so far from *firing firſt* upon the king's

troops; upon the most careful enquiry, it appears that but very few of our people fired at all; and even *they* did not fire 'till after being fired upon by the troops, they were wounded themselves, or saw others killed or wounded by them, and looked upon it next to impossible for them to escape.

As to any firing from the *meetinghouse*, as *Gage* represents; it is certain, that there were but *four men* in the *meetinghouse* when the troops came up: and they were then getting some ammunition from the town stock and had not so much as loaded their guns (except one, who never discharged it) when the troops fired upon the *militia*. And as to the *neighbouring houses*, it is equally certain that there was no firing from them, unless, after the dispersion of our men, some who had fled to them for shelter, might fire from them upon the troops.

One circumstance more, before the brigade quitted *Lexington*, I beg leave to mention, as what may give a further specimen of the *spirit* and *character*, of the officers and men of this body of troops. After the militia company were dispersed and the firing ceased, the troops drew up and formed in a body on the common, *fired a volley* and *gave three huzzas* by way of *triumph* and as expressive of the *joy of VIC-TORY* and *glory of CONQUEST!* Of this transaction I was a witness, having at that time a fair view of their motions and being at the distance of not more than 70 or 80 rods from them.

Whether this step was *honorary* to the detachment, or agreeable to the rules of war, or how far it was expressive of *bravery, heroism* and t*rue military glory*, for 800 disciplined troops of *Great Britain*, without notice or provocation, to fall upon 60 or 70 undisciplined *Americans*, who neither opposed nor molested them, and *murder* some and disperse the rest, and then to *give the shout* and *make the triumph of victory*, is not for me to determine, but must be submitted to the impartial world to judge. That "there is a God with whom is the power, and the glory, and the victory," is certain: but whether He will *set His seal* to the triumph made upon this most *peculiar* occasion, by following it with further successes and, finally giving up *this people* into the hands of those that have thus *cruelly* commenced hostilities against them, must be left to time to discover. But to return from this digression, if it may be called a digression.

Having thus *vanquished the party* in *Lexington*,

the troops marched on for *Concord* to execute their orders in destroying the stores belonging to the colony deposited there. They met with no interruption in their march to *Concord*. But by some means or other, the people of *Concord* had notice of their approach and designs, and were alarmed about break of day; and, collecting as soon and as many as possible, improved the time they had before the troops came upon them to the best advantage, both for concealing and securing as many of the public stores as they could, and in preparing for defence. By the stop of the troops at *Lexington*, many thousands were saved to the colony, and they were, in a great measure, frustrated in their design.

When the troops made their approach to the easterly part of the town, the provincials of *Concord* and some neighbouring towns were collected, and collecting, in an advantageous post on a hill a little distance from the *meetinghouse*, north of the road, to the number of about 150 or 200: but finding the troops to be more than three times as many, they wisely retreated, first to a hill about 80 rods further north, and then over the *north bridge* (so called) about a mile from town: and there they waited the

THE "MINUTE-MEN" OF THE REVOLUTION.

Published by Currier & Ives, NY, 1876

coming of the *militia,* of the towns adjacent, to their assistance.

In the meantime, the *British* detachment marched into the center of the town. A party of about 200 was ordered to take possession of *said bridge*; other parties were dispatched to various parts of the town in search of public stores, while the remainder were employed in seizing and destroying whatever they could find in the *townhouse* and other places where stores had been lodged. But before they had accomplished their design, they were interrupted by a discharge of arms at *said bridge*.

It seems, that of the party above-mentioned, as ordered to take possession of the bridge, one half were marched on about two miles in search of stores at *Col. Barret's* and that part of the town, while the other half, consisting of towards 100 men under *Capt. Lawrie,* were left to guard the bridge. The provincials who were in sight of the bridge, observing the troops attempting to take up the planks of said bridge, thought it necessary to dislodge them and gain possession of the bridge. They accordingly marched, but with express orders not to fire unless first fired upon by the king's troops. Upon their approach towards the bridge, *Capt. Lawrie's* party fired upon them, killed *Capt. Davis* and another man dead upon the spot, and wounded several others. Upon this, our *militia* rushed on with a spirit becoming *free-born Americans*, returned the fire upon the enemy, killed two, wounded several, and drove them from the bridge and pursued them towards the town 'till they were covered by a reinforcement from the main body. The provincials then took post on a hill at some distance north of the town: and as their numbers were continually increasing, they were preparing to give the troops a *proper discharge* on their departure from the town.

In the meantime, the king's troops collected; and having dressed their wounded, destroyed what stores they could find, and insulted and plundered a number of the inhabitants, prepared for a retreat.

"While at *Concord*, the troops disabled two 24 pounders; destroyed their two carriages and seven wheels for the same with their limbers. Sixteen wheels for brass 3-pounders, and two carriages with limber and wheels for two 4-pounders. They threw into the river, wells, &c., about 500 weight of ball: and stole about 60 barrels of flour; but not having time to perfect their work, one half of the flour was afterwards saved." [14]

The troops began a hasty retreat about the middle of the day and were no sooner out of town, but they began to meet the effects of the just resentments of this injured people. The provincials fired upon them from various quarters and pursued them (though without any military order) with a firmness and intrepidity, beyond what could have been expected on the first onset and in such a day of confusion and distress! The fire was returned, for a time, with great fury by the troops as they retreated, though (through divine goodness) with but little execution. This scene continued, with but little intermission, 'till they returned to *Lexington*, when it was evident, that, having lost numbers in killed, wounded, and prisoners that fell into our hands, they began to be not only fatigued, but greatly disheartened. And it is supposed they must have surrendered at discretion, had they not been reinforced. But *Lord Percy's* arrival with another brigade of about 1000 men and two field pieces, about half a mile from *Lexington meetinghouse*, towards *Cambridge*, gave them a seasonable respite.

The coming of the reinforcement with *the cannon*

(which our people were not so well acquainted with then as they have been since), put the provincials also to a pause for a time. But no sooner were the king's troops in motion, but our men renewed the pursuit with equal and even greater ardor and intrepidity than before, and the firing on both sides continued with but little intermission to the close of the day when the troops entered *Charlestown*, where the *provincials* could not follow them without exposing the worthy inhabitants of that *truly patriotic town* to their rage and revenge. That night and the next day, they were conveyed in boats over *Charles River* to *Boston*, glad to secure themselves under the cover of the shipping, and by strengthening and perfecting their fortifications at every part against further attacks of a justly incensed people, who, upon intelligence of the *murderous transactions* of this fatal day, were collecting in arms 'round the town in great numbers and from every quarter.

In the retreat of the king's troops from *Concord* to *Lexington*, they ravaged and plundered as they had opportunity, more or less, in most of the houses that were upon the road. But after they were joined by *Percy's brigade* in *Lexington*, it seemed as if *all the little remains* of humanity had left them; and rage and revenge had taken the reins and knew no bounds! *Clothing, furniture, provisions, goods, plundered, broken, carried off or destroyed! Buildings (especially dwelling houses) abused, defaced, battered, shattered and almost ruined! And as if this had not been enough, numbers of them doomed to the flames! Three dwelling houses, two shops, and a barn were laid in ashes in Lexington!*[15] *Many others were set on fire in this town, in Cambridge, &c., and must have shared the same fate had not the close pursuit of the provincials prevented, and the flames been seasonably quenched! Add to all this; the unarmed, the aged and infirm, who were unable to flee are inhumanly*

THE FIGHT AT CONCORD BRIDGE, APRIL 19, 1775

*stabbed and murdered in their habitations! Yea, even women in child bed with their helpless babes in their arms do not escape the horrid alternative of being either cruelly murdered in their beds, burnt in their habitations, or turned into the streets to perish with cold, nakedness and distress!* [16] *But I forbear: Words are too insignificant to express the horrid barbarities of that distressing day!* [17]

Our loss, in the several actions of that day, was 49 killed, 34 wounded and 5 missing, who were taken prisoners and have since been exchanged. The enemy's loss, according to the best accounts, in killed, wounded and missing, about 300.

As the war was thus begun with *savage cruelty* in the aggressors, so it has been carried on with the same temper and spirit by the enemy in but too many instances. Witness the *wanton cruelty*, discovered in burning *Charlestown, Norfolk, Falmouth, &c.* But as events which have taken place since the *ever memorable nineteenth of April*, 1775, do not properly come within the compass of this narrative, they must be left for some abler pen to relate.

## FINIS

# *Endnotes*

1 The event of this bold attempt was happy. A just and faithful God crowned the measures of the *confederate states* with success beyond their most sanguine expectations. The *church* was rescued from the darkness and error in which it had been involved for several hundred years before. A *glorious reformation* took place, which, in a good measure, restored the Christian religion to its ancient purity and native simplicity in many principal states and kingdoms in Europe. And a foundation was laid for rescuing the civil liberties of individuals, societies, states and kingdoms, as well as the common rights of mankind, from the *iron hand* of tyranny, the good effects of which was felt by the protestant states and kingdoms for several ages succeeding and are not totally lost, as to some, even at the present day though more than two centuries since. By this important *confederacy* of the *protestant powers* in Europe, it is evident that under providence, the power of the *beast* and the *false prophet* received a shock which it hath never recovered, the papal power both in church and state having been upon the decline from that time to this.

2 It is worthy of remark, that when the *Spanish court* undertook the subjugation of the *Dutch provinces in the Netherlands*, *Spain* was in the most respectable state it had been for a long time, having just concluded a victorious war and being then at peace with all the world.

At the same time, *Spain* had the best regulated army in Europe, commanded by the renowned *Duke of Alva*, the most experienced *General* then upon the stage. This wise, experienced and victorious *General* with his veteran, victorious troops was sent by the *Monarch* and court of Spain (like *Gage to Boston*) upon the *wholesome* and *pacific* business of supporting government in the *Dutch* provinces and enforcing obedience to what were called the laws of the kingdom or the mandates of their sovereign. Accordingly, after renewed injuries and repeated insults and cruelties, which rather invigorated than disheartened the *free* and *truly noble* spirits of the *Dutch*, at last it came to blood! The contest was, as might be expected, *long* and *bitter!* But under every disadvantage but the righteousness of their cause, they rose superior to their mighty and numerous oppressors; and heaven, at length, decided in their favour, crowned their endeavors with desired success, and gave and established unto them that *freedom* and *independence* for which they had so *bravely fought* and so *freely bled*. This freedom and independence so dearly purchased, they well knew how to prize and preserve; and by the smiles of heaven upon the wisdom and policy of their government, they have now enjoyed the blessings thereof, with but little interruption from enemies abroad or factions at home, for near two hundred years: And, in proportion to the extent of their territories and the number of inhabitants, they are, at this very time, justly esteemed one of the richest and most flourishing states in Europe. Thus hath a righteous God been pleased to plead their cause, and *cleanse* and *avenge* their *innocent blood*; and set them free from the oppressor's hand. Is not the cause of *Americans* equally just? Is not their God the same?

3 This refers to the *horrid massacre* in *Boston* on the evening of the 5th of March, 1770, when the guards under the command of *Capt. Preston* fired upon the inhabitants in King Street, killed 5 persons upon the spot, and wounded a number of others, several of whom afterwards died of their wounds!

4 A detachment from the *troops* then at *Danvers*, actually marched by *Gage's* order into the town of *Salem*, with orders (as it was said) to fire upon the inhabitants if they refused to disperse. But, as it happened, they had accomplished the affairs upon which they met before the troops arrived and even before they knew of their approach. This happily prevented the troops the opportunity of executing their orders and of *shedding of blood*, for that time.

5 This seizure of the stores, &c., roused the people more than anything that had happened before. Accordingly, the next day, viz. Sept. 2, 1774, *several thousands* not of the *rabble*, as *ministerial hirelings* have been disposed to speak, but of the respectable freeholders and free men of the adjacent towns collected at *Cambridge*; and to show their resentment at such *hostile measures* and their determined resolution never to submit to the *oppressive acts* without tumult or outrage, called *Lieut. Governor Oliver* and a number more of the *mandamus counsellors* before them and invited them to resign their seats at the board and to declare in a very solemn manner that they never would hold any office or post by virtue of said acts. The gentlemen applied to, complied with their proposals to general satisfaction.

Whether this step of the people was prudent and justifiable or not, it served to discover their sentiments of the acts of which they complained and their determined resolution to oppose them: And this was the main thing aimed at by the steps they took upon this occasion.

6 *Gen. Gage* repeatedly declared in his answers to the remonstrances of the town of *Boston*, the county of *Worcester* and the *Provincial Congress*, that he had no hostile intentions in any of these measures. With what truth and sincerity the *General* made such declarations, his after conduct fully determined.

7 This unsuccessful expedition was made on the LORD's day, Feb. 26, 1775. The party consisted of about 200 or 300 men; it was commanded by *Lieut. Col. Leslie.* The vessels which brought them to *Marblehead* arrived in the harbour on the morning of the Sabbath; and the better to conceal their intentions lay quietly at anchor near to the wharves with but very few hands upon deck (the troops being kept close) 'till the people of the town were assembled for the services of religion. While the inhabitants were thus engaged in their devotions to GOD, the party landed and made a speedy march to *Salem*. But all their precautions did not avail them for the accomplishment of their enterprise. The *eagle-eyes* of a watchful and wary people, justly jealous of every measure of their oppressors, were not easily evaded. Their motions were observed and such timely notice given, that such numbers were collected and such measures taken before they arrived, as effectually frustrated their design and obliged them to return defeated and chagrined.

8 The field (not of battle) but of *murder* and *bloodshed*, where our men were fired upon by the troops.

9 The persons killed in the morning when hostilities were first commenced were Messieurs *Robert Munroe*,

*Jonas Parker, Samuel Hadley, Jonathan Harrington, jr., Isaac Muzzy, Caleb Harrington* and John Brown, of *Lexington*; and one *Mr. Porter*, of *Woburn*. Wounded: *Jedediah Munro, Thomas Winship, Nathaniel Farmer, John Robbins, Solomon Pierce, John Tidd, Joseph Comee, Ebenezer Munroe, jr.*, and *Prince*, a Negro of *Lexington*, and *Jacob Bacon*, of *Woburn*. Afternoon, Killed: *Jedediah Munro, John Raymonds,* and *Nathaniel Wyman*. Wounded, in pursuit of the enemy, when retreating, *Francis Brown*. All of *Lexington*.

10  For the names of the killed and wounded, see note 9.

11  1200 or 1500 was the number we then supposed the brigade to consist of: though afterwards, by the best accounts, it appeared that there were but about 800.

12  From a most intimate acquaintance with the sentiments of the inhabitants of this town, then collected in arms, I think I may boldly assert that it was their *known* determination not to commence hostilities upon the king's troops; though they were equally determined to stand by their rights to the last.

13  See narrative and depositions, published by authority.

14  See *Rev. Mr. Gordon's* account.

15  Deacon Loring's house and barn, *Mrs. Lydia Mulliken's* house, and her son's shop, and *Mr. Joshua Bond's* house and shop.

16  See depositions published by authority.

17  *"Quorum parta magna sui!"* Virgil.

Henry Hudson Kitson, Sculptor

THE BEQUEST
OF
FRANCIS BROWN HAYES
TO
THE TOWN OF LEXINGTON
ERECTED 1899.

# *Appendix*

*Paul Revere's Ride*
—Henry Wadsworth Longfellow

*Lexington*
—Oliver Wendell Holmes

*Lexington*
—John Greenleaf Whittier

*Concord Hymn*
("shot heard round the world")
—Ralph Waldo Emerson

ONE OF THE LANTERNS THAT SIGNALED
PAUL REVERE'S RIDE APRIL 18, 1775,
CONCORD ANTIQUARIAN SOCIETY,
CONCORD, MASSACHUSETTS

[General Gage, hearing that Samuel Adams and John Hancock would be at Lexington, came with 800 men to arrest them for treason, with intention to destroy munitions at Concord also. Joseph Warren discerned his purpose and informed Paul Revere to spread a warning.   —Editor]

## PAUL REVERE'S RIDE
[April 18–19, 1775]

LISTEN, my children, and you shall hear
Of the midnight ride of Paul Revere,
On the eighteenth of April, in Seventy-five;
Hardly a man is now alive
Who remembers that famous day and year.

He said to his friend, "If the British march
By land or sea from the town tonight,
Hang a lantern aloft in the belfry arch
Of the North Church tower as a signal light —
One, if by land, and two, if by sea;
And I on the opposite shore will be,
Ready to ride and spread the alarm
Through every Middlesex village and farm,
For the country folk to be up and to arm."

Then he said, "Good night!" and with muffled oar
Silently rowed to the Charlestown shore,
Just as the moon rose over the bay,
Where swinging wide at her moorings lay
The *Somerset*, British man-of-war;
A phantom ship, with each mast and spar
Across the moon like a prison bar,
And a huge black hulk, that was magnified
By its own reflection in the tide.

Meanwhile, his friend, through alley and street,
Wanders and watches with eager ears,
Till in the silence around him he hears
The muster of men at the barrack door,
The sound of arms, and the tramp of feet,
And the measured tread of the grenadiers,
Marching down to their boats on the shore.

Then he climbed the tower of the Old North Church,
By the wooden stairs, with stealthy tread,
To the belfry-chamber overhead,
And startled the pigeons from their perch
On the somber rafters, that round him made
Masses and moving shapes of shade —
By the trembling ladder, steep and tall,
To the highest window in the wall,
Where he paused to listen and look down
A moment on the roofs of the town,
And the moonlight flowing over all.

Beneath, in the churchyard, lay the dead,
In their night-encampment on the hill,
Wrapped in silence so deep and still
That he could hear, like a sentinel's tread,
The watchful night-wind, as it went
Creeping along from tent to tent,
And seeming to whisper, "All is well!"
A moment only he feels the spell
Of the place and the hour, and the secret dread
Of the lonely belfry and the dead;
For suddenly all his thoughts are bent
On a shadowy something far away,
Where the river widens to meet the bay—
A line of black that bends and floats
On the rising tide, like a bridge of boats.

Meanwhile, impatient to mount and ride,
Booted and spurred, with a heavy stride
On the opposite shore walked Paul Revere.
Now he patted his horse's side,
Now gazed at the landscape far and near,
Then, impetuous, stamped the earth,
And turned and tightened his saddle-girth;
But mostly he watched with eager search
The belfry-tower of the Old North Church,
As it rose above the graves on the hill,
Lonely and spectral and somber and still.
And lo! as he looks, on the belfry's height
A glimmer, and then a gleam of light!

He springs to the saddle, the bridle he turns,
But lingers and gazes, till full on his sight
A second lamp in the belfry burns!

A hurry of hoofs in a village ſtreet,
A shape in the moonlight, a bulk in the dark,
And beneath, from the pebbles, in passing, a spark
Struck out by a ſteed flying fearless and fleet:
That was all! And yet, through the gloom and the light,
The fate of a nation was riding that night;
And the spark ſtruck out by that ſteed, in his flight,
Kindled the land into flame with its heat.

He has left the village and mounted the ſteep,
And beneath him, tranquil and broad and deep,
Is the Myſtic, meeting the ocean tides;
And under the alders that skirt its edge,
Now soft on the sand, now loud on the ledge,
Is heard the tramp of his ſteed as he rides.

It was twelve by the village clock,
When he crossed the bridge into Medford Town.
He heard the crowing of the cock,
And the barking of the farmer's dog,
And felt the damp of the river fog,
That rises after the sun goes down.

It was one by the village clock,
When he galloped into Lexington.
He saw the gilded weathercock
Swim in the moonlight as he passed,
And the meeting-house windows, blank and bare,
Gaze at him with a spectral glare,
As if they already stood aghast
At the bloody work they would look upon.

It was two by the village clock,
When he came to the bridge in Concord Town.
He heard the bleating of the flock,
And the twitter of birds among the trees,
And felt the breath of the morning breeze
Blowing over the meadows brown.
And one was safe and asleep in his bed
Who at the bridge would be first to fall,
Who that day would be lying dead,
Pierced by a British musket-ball.

You know the rest. In the books you have read,
How the British Regulars fired and fled —
How the farmers gave them ball for ball,
From behind each fence and farm-yard wall,
Chasing the red-coats down the lane,
Then crossing the fields to emerge again
Under the trees at the turn of the road,
And only pausing to fire and load.

So through the night rode Paul Revere;
And so through the night went his cry of alarm
To every Middlesex village and farm—
A cry of defiance and not of fear,
A voice in the darkness, a knock at the door,
And a word that shall echo forevermore!
For, borne on the night-wind of the Past,
Through all our history, to the last,
In the hour of darkness and peril and need,
The people will waken and listen to hear
The hurrying hoof-beats of that steed,
And the midnight message of Paul Revere.

—HENRY WADSWORTH LONGFELLOW

## LEXINGTON
### [April 19, 1775]

Slowly the mist o'er the meadow was creeping,
   Bright on the dewy buds glistened the sun,
When from his couch, while his children were sleeping,
   Rose the bold rebel and shouldered his gun.
     Waving her golden veil
     Over the silent dale,
Blithe looked the morning on cottage and spire;
     Hushed was his parting sigh,
     While from his noble eye
Flashed the last sparkle of liberty's fire.

On the smooth green where the fresh leaf is springing
   Calmly the first-born of glory have met;
Hark! the death-volley around them is ringing!
   Look! with their life-blood the young grass is wet!
     Faint is the feeble breath,
     Murmuring low in death,
"Tell to our sons how their fathers have died";
     Nerveless the iron hand,
     Raised for its native land,
Lies by the weapon that gleams at its side.

Over the hillsides the wild knell is tolling,
    From their far hamlets the yeomanry come;
As through the storm-clouds the thunder-burst rolling,
    Circles the beat of the mustering drum.
        Fast on the soldier's path
        Darken the waves of wrath —
Long have they gathered and loud shall they fall;
        Red glares the musket's flash,
        Sharp rings the rifle's crash,
Blazing and clanging, from thicket and wall.

Gayly the plume of the horseman was dancing,
    Never to shadow his cold brow again;
Proudly at morning the war-steed was prancing,
    Reeking and panting he droops on the rein;
        Pale is the lip of scorn,
        Voiceless the trumpet horn,
Torn is the silken-fringed red cross on high;
        Many a belted breast
        Low on the turf shall rest
Ere the dark hunters the herd have passed by.

Snow-girdled crags where the hoarse wind is raving,
    Rocks where the wear floods murmur and wail,
Wilds where the fern by the furrow is waving,
    Reeled with the echoes that rode on the gale;
        Far as the tempest thrills
        Over the darkened hills,
Far as the sunshine streams over the plain,
        Roused by the tyrant band,
        Woke all the mighty land,
Girdled for battle, from mountain to main.

Green be the graves where her martyrs are lying!
   Shroudless and tombless they sunk to their rest,
While o'er their ashes the starry fold flying
   Wraps the proud eagle they roused from his nest.
      Borne on her Northern pine,
      Long o'er the foaming brine
Spread her broad banner to storm and to sun;
      Heaven keep her ever free,
      Wide as o'er land and sea
Floats the fair emblem her heroes have won!
                —OLIVER WENDELL HOLMES

[Thanks to the advance warnings, before the British could reach Concord, the amunitions were hidden. As more minute-men came to fight, and finally made a stand at the Concord Bridge, the British were forced to retreat, under fire from trees and hedges all day along their path from Concord to Boston, leaving 273 British and 93 Americans killed.    —Editor]

## LEXINGTON
### [1775]

No berserk thirst of blood had they,
     No battle-joy was theirs, who set
     Against the alien bayonet
Their homespun breasts in that old day.

Their feet had trodden peaceful ways;
     They loved not strife, they dreaded pain;
     They saw not, what to us is plain,
That God would make man's wrath His praise.

No seers were they, but simple men;
      Its vast results the future hid:
      The meaning of the work they did
Was strange and dark and doubtful then.

Swift as their summons came they left
      The plow mid-furrow standing still,
      The half-ground corn grist in the mill,
The spade in earth, the axe in cleft.

They went where duty seemed to call,
      They scarcely asked the reason why;
      They only knew they could but die,
And death was not the worst of all!

Detail from a 19th century engraving based on the painting by John Trumbull finished in 1786.

Of man for man the sacrifice,
    All that was theirs to give, they gave.
    The flowers that blossomed from their grave
Have sown themselves beneath all skies.

Their death-shot shook the feudal tower,
    And shattered slavery's chain as well;
    On the sky's dome, as on a bell,
Its echo struck the world's great hour.

That fateful echo is not dumb:
    The nations listening to its sound
    Wait, from a century's vantage-ground,
The holier triumphs yet to come —

The bridal time of Law and Love,
    The gladness of the world's release,
    When, war-sick, at the feet of Peace
The hawk shall nestle with the dove! —

The golden age of brotherhood
    Unknown to other rivalries
    Than of the mild humanities,
And gracious interchange of good,

When closer strand shall lean to strand,
    Till meet, beneath saluting flags,
    The eagle of our mountain-crags,
The lion of our Motherland!
                    —JOHN GREENLEAF WHITTIER

[Ralph Waldo Emerson composed this special poem for the dedication of the monument to mark the location of the first battle of the Revolution and commemorate "the shot heard round the world." —Editor]

# Concord Hymn

## Sung at the Completion
## of the Battle Monument
April 19, 1836

By THE rude bridge that arched the flood,
  Their flag to April's breeze unfurled,
Here once the embattled farmers stood,
  And fired the shot heard round the world.

The foe long since in silence slept;
  Alike the conqueror silent sleeps;
And Time the ruined bridge has swept
  Down the dark stream which seaward creeps.

On this green bank, by this soft stream,
  We set today a votive stone;
That memory may their deed redeem,
  When, like our sires, our sons are gone.

Spirit that made those heroes dare
  To die, and leave their children free,
Bid Time and Nature gently spare
  The shaft we raise to them and thee.

—RALPH WALDO EMERSON

*The*
*End*

# More from Nordskog Publishing, Inc.

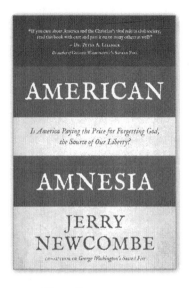

## AMERICAN AMNESIA

*Is America Paying the Price for Forgetting God, the Source of Our Liberty?*

DR. JERRY NEWCOMBE, DMIN continues to press the cause of Christ through his powerful commentary on current affairs from a Biblical worldview with his latest book, a compilation of his essays syndicated on outlets such as *WorldNetDaily*, *Newsmax*, *Christian Post*, *Town Hall*, djameskennedy.org, & others.

## THE BOOK THAT MADE AMERICA

*How the Bible Formed Our Nation*

by DR. JERRY NEWCOMBE, DMIN

Not long ago, President Obama declared that America is not a Christian nation, while Newsweek announced the demise of Christian America. Yet, in truth, all that is positive in our foundation can be traced back to the Scriptures. This book is the answer to America's critics, using the facts of history.

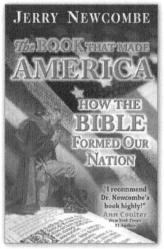

 **Nordskog** Publishing Inc.

NordskogPublishing.com

2716 Sailor Avenue, Ventura, California 93001 1-805-642-2070 • 1-805-276-5129

# More from Nordskog Publishing, Inc.

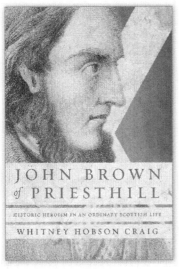

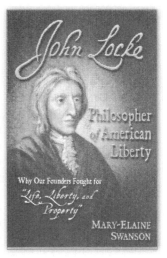

**Nordskog** Publishing™

NordskogPublishing.com

2716 Sailor Avenue, Ventura, California 93001 1-805-642-2070 • 1-805-276-5129

# More from Nordskog Publishing, Inc.

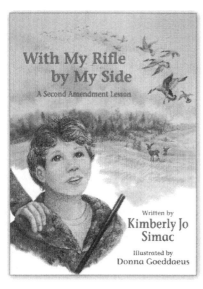
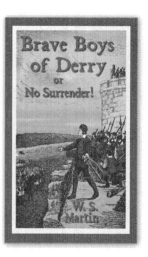

# More from Nordskog Publishing, Inc.

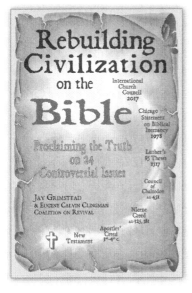

## REBUILDING CIVILIZATION ON THE BIBLE
*Proclaiming the Truth on 24 Controversial Issues*

by **JAY GRIMSTEAD &
EUGENE CALVIN CLINGMAN,**
*Coalition on Revival*

Anything that waters down, neglects, or rejects God's Word as the sole source of ultimate truth undermines the faith of Jesus Christ in the world. In *Rebuilding Civilization*, Jay Grimstead uses historic tools to answer 24 controversial doctrinal questions, defending the historic Biblical faith with Scripture.

## THE FOUR IN ONE GOSPEL OF JESUS
*Chronologically Integrated According to Matthew, Mark, Luke, and John*

Compiled by **NIKOLA DIMITROV**

*Four in One* is, word for word, a harmony of the four Biblical Gospels rearranged into a single chronological narrative according to the best scholarship. Matthew, Mark, Luke, and John fully represent God and themselves in this faithful Gospel book, perfect for seekers, new believers, and scholars alike.

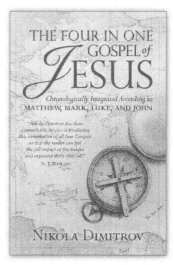

 **Nordskog** Publishing inc.

**NordskogPublishing.com**
2716 Sailor Avenue, Ventura, California 93001  1-805-642-2070 • 1-805-276-5129

To see all of our exciting titles,
view book contents, and order ebooks
go to:
NordskogPublishing.com

If you like FREE *information* and *juicy* content,
you are in for enjoyment, insight, and
inspiration via our **eNewsletter,**
***The Bell Ringer.***
Sign up here:
NordskogPublishing.com/media/

Browse articles, poems, and testimonies
by various perceptive writers, at
NordskogPublishing.com/category/publishers-corner/

Ask the publisher about upcoming titles and
e-book versions, and a discount when you
purchase multiple books.